HOW TO SAVE MONEY WHILE SHOPPING ONLINE

STRATEGIES FOR SAVING MONEY WHILE SHOPPING ONLINE

CYRIL LAKES

Contents

CHAPTER ONE

Overview

The way individuals shop for goods and services has been completely transformed by online purchasing, or e-commerce. It entails utilizing a computer, smartphone, or other internet-connected device to make purchases of goods or services over the internet while at home or on the move. The emergence of e-commerce has revolutionized the retail sector by providing customers with unprecedented levels of convenience, choice, and accessibility.

Important Online Shopping Facts:

Convenience: This is one of the main benefits of shopping online. Without having to visit actual stores, customers can browse a wide selection of products, compare prices, read reviews, and make purchases whenever and wherever they choose with just a few clicks.

Large Selection: The variety of products available for purchase online come from all around the world. Customers have a wide range of selections, frequently more than traditional brick-and-mortar retailers, to pick from when buying food, electronics, apparel, or specialty items.

Price Comparison: Customers may easily locate the best offers and discounts by comparing prices from other merchants when they shop online. To assist customers in saving money, numerous websites and applications also provide price-tracking features and alerts.

Concierge Services: Based on a customer's browsing history and interests, several online businesses provide customized suggestions and concierge services. These services improve the shopping experience by offering support and personalized product recommendations.

Convenient Payment Options: Digital wallets, credit/debit cards, and online payment gateways are just a few of the convenient payment options that e-commerce platforms provide. Customers can select the payment method that best fits their needs and preferences thanks to this flexibility.

Doorstep Delivery: The convenience of doorstep delivery is one of the best things about internet buying. Online shoppers save time and don't have to go to real stores because their purchases are delivered right to their home.

Customer Reviews and Ratings: Customer reviews and ratings are a common element of online buying platforms. They offer insightful information about the suitability, effectiveness, and contentment of a specific product. Customers can use this information to make well-informed purchases.

24/7 Accessibility: Online shopping platforms are available around-the-clock, seven days a week, in contrast to traditional establishments that have set business hours. Customers can shop whenever it's most convenient for them, whether it's on the weekends or in the early morning hours.

Return and Exchange Policies: A lot of internet merchants provide simple return and exchange procedures, enabling clients to send back or swap out goods that don't live up to their expectations. This lowers the danger involved with internet purchase and gives comfort.

All things considered, internet shopping provides unmatched choice, flexibility, and convenience, making it a decision that people all over the world are choosing more and more. The online shopping experience is anticipated to grow even more smooth and customized as technology advances, significantly improving how consumers purchase for goods and services in the digital era.

Comparative Buying

Before making a purchase, consumers engage in a habit known as comparison shopping, which involves comparing the costs, features, and quality of goods and services offered by various brands and shops. Customers can use this technique to compare prices and make well-informed decisions based on their needs and preferences. An outline of comparison shopping is provided below:

Goal:

The main objective of comparison shopping is to find the best offer or value for a specific good or service.

Customers may make sure they're getting the best value for their money and steer clear of overpaying for goods or services by comparing costs, features, and reviews.

Techniques:

Online comparison tools: Customers can compare costs from several brands or merchants by using a variety of websites and apps that offer comparison features. These platforms frequently compile product listings from several sources and display them in a manner that makes comparisons simple.

In-Store Comparison: Before making a choice, some customers would rather compare items face-to-face by visiting a number of actual locations to evaluate features, costs, and quality.

Word-of-mouth suggestions: Consumers can also obtain information about goods and services and contrast their experiences with various brands or merchants by asking friends, family, or online groups for suggestions.

Things to Take Into Account:

Price: The cost of the good or service is by far the most important consideration when doing a price comparison. Shoppers search for the greatest deal by comparing prices offered by various retailers.

Quality: Consumers look at the dependability and quality of goods and services in addition to pricing. This could be looking through product details, reading reviews, or evaluating the retailer's or brand's reputation.

Features: Depending on the type of product, buyers can evaluate features, technical details, and functionality to decide which one best suits their requirements.

Extra Costs: When doing a comparison shop, it's important to take into account other expenses like taxes, shipping charges, return policies, and warranties since these may affect the final cost of the item.

Advantages:

Savings: By locating sales, special offers, or less expensive options, comparison shopping assists customers in making financial savings.

Well-Informed Decisions: Customers can make well-informed decisions that fit their needs, wants, and budget by obtaining information and contrasting possibilities.

Confidence: Knowing they've considered a range of possibilities and chosen the best one for their circumstances, customers who comparison shop are more confident in their purchases.

CHAPTER TWO

Problems:

Time and Effort: Comparing prices across various stores can take a lot of time and effort, particularly when looking at a variety of goods or services.

Information Overload: With so many options at their disposal, consumers could feel overloaded with information to sort through and consider.

Bias and Misinformation: To avoid biased product reviews or deceptive product descriptions, consumers should exercise caution when obtaining information from internet sources.

Overall, by comparing prices, features, and quality, comparison shopping enables customers to make informed judgments about what to buy. Through the utilization of diverse tools and resources, buyers can proficiently explore the market and identify the optimal bargain for their requirements.

Making Use of Promo Codes and Coupons

One great method to lower the cost of online shopping and save money on your purchases is to use coupons and promo codes. Here's how to use promo codes and coupons to get the most out of your purchases:

Look for promo codes and coupons:

Prior to making a purchase, start by looking for coupons and promo codes online. Coupon websites, retailer emails, social networking platforms, and retailer loyalty programs are some places you can get these codes.

Seek out websites that are experts in compiling discount coupons and promo codes from different merchants so that finding deals on particular goods or establishments is simple.

Verify Expiration Dates and Restrictions:

Make sure the restrictions and conditions of any discount or promo code apply to your purchase before using it.

Keep an eye out for any restrictions, such as time limits on using the coupon, prohibitions on specific brands or products, or minimum purchase requirements.

Remember the expiration date and use the promo code or coupon before it ends to receive the discounted price.

Use codes while checking out:

When you're prepared to buy, visit the retailer's website and go to the checkout page.

Find a field that says "promo code," "coupon code," or "discount code" so that you may enter the code you've discovered there.

To see the discount reflected in the total of your order, accurately enter the code and click "apply".

Mix promo codes and coupons:

You may stack coupons or promo codes at certain retailers to get even more discounts. Try using your codes in combination if you have more than one that can be used to receive the most discount.

Remember that stacking codes are not always allowed by merchants, so make sure to review the terms and restrictions in advance.

Enroll in Reward Programs:

Numerous retailers have loyalty plans and rewards programs that grant members access to exclusive discounts, promo codes, and coupons.

To take advantage of extra savings opportunities and to be informed about upcoming discounts, think about enrolling in these programs.

Join Retailers' Social Media Followings:

Retailers frequently post promo codes, flash sales, and special discounts on their social media platforms.

Stay up to date on the newest sales and discounts by following your preferred stores on social media sites like Facebook, Twitter, and Instagram.

Make Use of Browser Add-ons:

You can save time and effort at checkout by having browser extensions like Honey, Rakuten, or RetailMeNot automatically discover and apply appropriate coupons and promo codes.

Remain Prepared:

Organize the coupons and discount codes that you have found and intend to utilize in a spreadsheet or note-taking tool.

To make sure you utilize the codes before they expire, set reminders for the dates of expiration.

You may successfully use coupons and promo codes to lower the cost of online buying and take advantage of large savings on your purchases by adhering to these pointers and techniques.

Making the Most of Reward Schemes

By using rewards programs when you shop online, you can have access to special privileges, save money, and get discounts. Here's how to maximize rewards programs for online shopping:

Enroll in Several Programs:

Look through a variety of stores and online stores to discover rewards programs that suit your tastes and purchasing routines.

To increase your earning potential, think about enrolling in loyalty programs provided by credit card issuers, cashback websites, and your favorite stores.

Recognize the Benefits of the Program:

Learn about the advantages provided by each rewards program, like the ability to accrue points, receive cashback, receive special discounts, receive free shipping, receive birthday presents, or access early to deals.

Read the terms and conditions carefully, taking note of any limitations, deadlines, or minimum expenditure requirements.

Connect Cards and Accounts:

To make sure you get rewarded automatically when you shop online, link your rewards program accounts to your payment processors or online shopping accounts.

Certain credit card issuers provide bonus benefits for spending on certain things, such groceries, dining out, or internet shopping. When making purchases online, make use of credit cards that provide the biggest benefits.

Utilize rewards portals when making purchases:

A lot of reward programs include connections with retailers or online shopping portals where you may earn cashback or additional points for purchases made on their platform.

To earn rewards on your transaction, visit the retailer's website via the rewards portal of your preferred program before making a purchase.

Benefit from Bonus Offers:

Watch out for exclusive offers, bonuses, or time-limited promotions that let you get more incentives for doing particular things, including buying something for the first time, recommending friends, or finishing a certain amount of transactions.

To be informed about upcoming promotions and chances to earn additional rewards, choose to receive email notifications or alerts from your rewards programs.

Combine promo codes and coupons with rewards:

Combine loyalty program incentives with merchant coupons, promo codes, or discounts to get the most out of your savings.

Seek chances to combine rewards with additional cost-cutting techniques to increase the total amount you save on purchases.

Monitor and Utilize Awards:

Utilize the rewards program's website or mobile app to monitor your reward earnings, point balance, and redemption choices.

Keep an eye on the expiration dates of your points and seize any chances to exchange them for money, gift cards, merchandise, or travel before they run out.

Give Input and Take Part in Surveys:

Certain reward schemes give extra points or incentives for doing surveys, giving feedback, or interacting with the company on social media.

Utilize these chances to share your thoughts and experiences with the shop and win further prizes.

Engaging in rewards programs and taking advantage of its advantages can improve your online shopping experience, help you save money, and provide you access to exclusive bonuses and discounts.

When to Make Purchases

It's true that you can optimize your savings and lower the cost of internet shopping by strategically timing your purchases. Here are some pointers for efficiently timing your purchases:

Track Sales Cycles:

Retailers sometimes run sales cycles during which they give discounts on particular product categories or at particular times of the year.

Observe these cycles of sales and schedule your purchases appropriately. For instance, apparel may experience markdowns at the conclusion of each season, while electronics typically go on sale around Black Friday and Cyber Monday.

Benefit from Seasonal Sales:

Seasonal sales and promotions are widely offered by merchants as a means of reducing inventory and creating space for new arrivals.

To find reduced things, look for end-of-season bargains, holiday sales, and special occasions like back-to-school or clearance sales.

Look out for daily deals and flash sales:

Look out for retailer flash discounts and daily deals, where items are marked down significantly for a brief period of time.

Join email newsletter subscription services or follow shops on social media to get updated about these limited-time sales.

Shop Off-Season Hours:

Steer clear of busy weekends, holidays, and major shopping occasions when there is a lot of demand and a chance of price inflation.

Rather, think about going shopping at off-peak hours, including late at night or on weekday mornings, when stores could be more willing to give special discounts or lower pricing to draw in people.

Employ Tools for Price Tracking:

Make use of price monitoring applications and browser extensions that keep track of price changes and alert you when the cost of goods you're interested in lower.

By using these tools, you can make sure you're receiving the best deal and determine when is the ideal time to buy.

Make a plan for significant sales occasions.

Make sure to put important sales dates on your calendar, such as Cyber Monday, Black Friday, Prime Day, or Singles' Day, when many stores offer substantial discounts and deals.

To get the greatest discounts on the things you want, make a list of things you want to buy in advance and wait for these occasions.

Mix Coupons and Discounts:

To optimize your savings, look for chances to stack coupons and discounts.

Certain stores provide even bigger savings on your entire order when you apply multiple discounts or promo codes on a single purchase.

Think About When to Make Large Purchases:

When buying expensive goods like electronics, furniture, or appliances, there can be substantial discounts to be had by timing your purchase.

Examine past pricing patterns and contemplate holding off on purchasing these things till after special occasions or bargains.

Profit from Price Matching Policies:

Certain retailers provide price matching programs, whereby they will match or surpass the pricing of comparable products offered by competitors.

Pay attention to what your competitors are charging and use price matching to make sure you're getting the greatest offer.

You can efficiently lower the cost of online shopping and optimize your savings by planning your purchases ahead of time and taking advantage of sales, promotions, and discounts.

CHAPTER THREE

Taking into Account Return and Shipping Policies

Reducing the cost of online buying and guaranteeing a positive shopping experience need careful consideration of shipping and return policies. To optimize savings, consider the following shipping and return policies:

Free Delivery Cutoff Points:

When an order reaches a specific minimum purchase amount, a lot of online shops provide free shipping. Check if the shop offers free shipping before making a purchase, and if not, think about adding more products to your cart to meet the minimum and save on postage.

Options for Shipping Speed:

Select the shipping option that best suits your demands and budget. If you are willing to wait a few extra days for delivery, choose standard shipping as it is frequently less expensive than expedited or express shipping.

Make Use of Free Shipping Offers:

Benefit from merchant deals and promotions that include free shipping. Plan your purchases appropriately by keeping an eye out for special offers, such as free shipping on weekends or holidays.

Ship to Locker or Store:

Certain retailers allow you to mail your order to a locker or nearby location for free pickup. This can reduce the cost of delivery and offer convenience, particularly if you're not eager to get your stuff.

Register and Keep Up with Programs:

Take into consideration signing up for retailer subscribe and save programs, which give free shipping on regular orders of necessities like food, personal care products, and household goods.

Examine the Returns Policy:

Check the retailer's return policy before making a purchase to make sure you are aware of the requirements for exchanges and returns.

To reduce the expense and inconvenience of returning things if necessary, look for merchants with flexible return policies that provide free returns, extended return windows, or in-store return options.

Consider Return Shipping Expenses:

If the store does not provide free returns, think about if the savings on the item are outweighed by the return shipping costs. When calculating the total cost of a purchase, especially for larger or heavier items, account for the cost of return postage.

Examine product descriptions and customer feedback:

Make sure the item fulfills your expectations and lowers the possibility that you will have to return it because you are not happy with it by carefully reading the product descriptions, specifications, and customer reviews.

Think about trading options:

Rather than accepting returns, some stores let you exchange an item for a different size, color, or style at no extra cost. Look into trade possibilities instead of sending things back for a refund.

Apply Shipping Labels for Returns:

If you do need to return an item, use the return shipping label that the retailer, if any, has given. When compared to organizing return shipment on your own, retailers frequently provide flat-rate return shipping labels or discounted shipping prices.

When you order online, take into account the shipping and return policies to save money on delivery, take advantage of free shipping offers, and make sure that returns are handled smoothly. You may shop with confidence and save as much money as possible on internet purchases thanks to this.

Registering for Alerts and Newsletters by Email

Several advantages that lower the cost of online purchasing might come from subscribing to email newsletters and notifications from online shops. These are a few of the benefits:

Exclusive Savings and Offers:

Retailers frequently give their email newsletter subscribers access to special offers, promo codes, and unique discounts. You may take advantage of these exclusive deals by signing up, which will enable you to make savings on your purchases.

Early Access to Sales:

Subscribers to email newsletters may obtain early access to sales events, allowing them to buy popular items before they sell out or before prices increase. This can give you a competitive edge and ensure you obtain the greatest discounts before they're gone.

Flash Sales and Limited-Time Offers:

Many retailers use email newsletters to announce flash deals and limited-time bargains that are only accessible for a short period. Subscribers receive information about these specials in advance, allowing them the opportunity to take advantage of lower pricing before they expire.

New Product Announcements:

Stay informed about the latest product releases, arrivals, and collections by subscribing to our newsletters. Retailers regularly send out newsletters to announce new products, allowing you to be among the first to find and purchase them.

Personalized Recommendations:

Some businesses utilize email newsletters to deliver personalized product recommendations based on your browsing history, buying behavior, and preferences. This might help you discover relevant products and uncover items that match your hobbies and style.

Birthday Discounts and Rewards:

Many retailers give birthday discounts or gifts to members of their email newsletters as a unique bonus. By submitting your birthdate when signing up, you may receive exclusive offers or discounts to honor your big day.

Information About Clearance Sales and Deals:

Stay updated on clearance sales, markdowns, and special deals by subscribing to email newsletters. Retailers often send out information about clearance events, allowing you to score lower prices on a wide range of products.

Insider Tips & Shopping Advice:

Get exclusive secrets, buying advice, and style inspiration from retailers through their email newsletters. Many newsletters contain helpful material such as fashion advice, product reviews, and gift ideas to assist you in making informed shopping decisions.

Free Shipping and Returns Offers:

Some retailers provide free shipping or returns deals solely to subscribers of their email newsletters. By joining up, you may receive special offers that assist cut shipping costs and make online purchasing more cheap.

Stay Connected with Your Favorite Brands:

Signing up for email newsletters allows you to stay connected with your favorite brands and merchants, receiving details about their latest items, events, and specials straight in your inbox.

Overall, subscribing to email newsletters and alerts from online merchants can give useful benefits that help you save money, remain informed, and enjoy a more pleasant online shopping experience.

Using Cashback and Rebate Websites

Using cashback and rebate websites is an excellent strategy to lower the cost of online shopping and get money back on your purchases. Here's how these platforms function and how they can help you save money:

Cashback on Purchases:

Cashback websites work with retailers to provide consumers a percentage of their purchase money back as cashback benefits.

When you shop through a cashback website, you earn a portion of your purchase value as cashback, which is paid into your account on the cashback platform.

reward rates vary depending on the shop and product category, with some offering higher reward rates than others.

Rebates and Coupons:

In addition to cashback benefits, some cashback services offer rebates and discounts that provide additional savings on purchases.

These rebates and coupons may be applied at checkout to reduce the cost of your order, allowing you to save even more money on your purchases.

Wide Selection of Retailers:

Cashback websites collaborate with a wide range of shops, including renowned online stores, department stores, travel websites, and more.

CHAPTER FOUR

This allows you to earn cashback benefits on a variety of purchases, from clothing and electronics to travel bookings and household supplies.

Easy to Use:

Using cashback and rebate websites is quick and straightforward. To earn cashback, you just join up for an account on the cashback platform, explore available offers, and click over to the retailer's website to make your purchase.

The cashback credits are immediately monitored and credited to your account, often within a few days or weeks after your transaction.

Stacking with Discounts and Promotions:

Cashback incentives can often be stacked with discounts, promo codes, and other promotions offered by shops, allowing you to optimize your savings on purchases.

This means you may still take advantage of specials, coupons, and other discounts offered by shops while receiving cashback on your purchases.

No Cost to Use:

Cashback and rebate websites are free to use and do not charge any fees or subscription costs. You just get cashback rewards on your purchases without any added expense.

Payout Options:

Most cashback websites offer numerous payout alternatives for claiming your cashback benefits, such as PayPal payouts, bank transfers, gift cards, or charitable donations.

You can choose the payout option that best meets your interests and needs.

Tracking and Monitoring:

Cashback websites provide tools and services to track and monitor your cashback earnings, including transaction history, pending cashback, and payout status.

This allows you to keep track of your earnings and guarantee that you receive the cashback benefits you're entitled to.

Overall, using cashback and rebate websites is a simple and effective approach to save money on online purchasing. By collecting cashback incentives on your purchases, you can minimize the cost of your orders and enjoy additional savings with no effort.

Employing Browser Extensions and Price Tracking Tools

Employing browser extensions and price tracking tools can be immensely effective for saving money while shopping online. Here's how:

Automatic Coupon and Promo Code Application:

Browser extensions like Honey or RetailMeNot automatically search for and apply relevant coupons and promo codes at checkout, saving you time and effort.

These extensions scan the web for available discounts and apply them to your order, letting you receive the best bargain possible without having to search for codes manually.

Price Comparison:

Browser extensions such as PriceBlink or InvisibleHand check prices across different merchants in real-time, displaying the best available prices for the goods you're viewing.

By comparing costs across several retailers, you can verify you're getting the lowest price available and avoid overpaying for things.

Deal Alerts & Notifications:

Price tracking programs like CamelCamelCamel or Keepa allow you to establish price alerts for certain products and receive messages when prices drop below a given threshold.

You'll be notified via email or browser notifications when the price of an item you're interested in falls, enabling you to capitalize on deals and save money.

Historical Price Data:

pricing tracking tools provide historical pricing data for products, allowing you to examine how prices have moved over time.

By reviewing price history, you can assess whether the present price is a good deal or if it's likely to drop more in the future, helping you make informed purchasing decisions.

Price History Charts:

Some price tracking programs offer price history charts that visualize pricing trends and changes for a given product.

These charts provide vital insights into pricing patterns and help you evaluate the ideal moment to buy, ensuring you obtain the lowest price possible.

Price Drop Alerts:

Price tracking programs offer price drop alerts, telling you when the price of a product you're tracking falls.

You can establish price drop thresholds and receive alerts when prices fall below your defined level, allowing you to take advantage of deals and save money.

Product Reviews and Ratings:

Some browser extensions and price tracking applications allow access to product reviews and ratings from other shoppers.

Reading reviews and ratings can help you make informed purchasing decisions and avoid buying products with poor quality or performance, thereby saving you money in the long term.

Browser Compatibility:

Browser extensions and price tracking tools are compatible with popular web browsers like Chrome, Firefox, and Safari, ensuring interoperability across numerous platforms and devices.

You can install these extensions on your choice browser and enjoy their capabilities easily while shopping online.

Overall, adopting browser extensions and price tracking tools can help you save money by automatically applying coupons and promo codes, comparing prices, receiving deal notifications, and accessing valuable insights into pricing patterns and product quality. By employing these tools, you may maximize your savings and make smarter purchasing selections when shopping online.

summary

In conclusion, saving money while shopping online is attainable through numerous tactics and technologies meant to assist consumers make informed purchasing decisions and acquire the greatest offers. By utilizing a combination of methods, customers can optimize their savings and stretch their budgets farther. Here's a breakdown of significant themes discussed:

Utilize Coupons and Promo Codes: Take advantage of discounts, coupons, and promo codes offered by shops to minimize the cost of your purchases.

Comparison Shopping: Compare prices across different retailers to ensure you're receiving the greatest deal possible. Use price comparison websites and browser extensions to ease the process.

Timing Your Purchases: Pay attention to sales cycles, seasonal promotions, and significant sales events to capitalize on discounts and special deals.

Consider Shipping and Return Policies: Factor in shipping expenses, return policies, and any associated fees when evaluating the total worth of a transaction.

Sign Up for Rewards Programs: Join rewards programs offered by merchants and credit card issuers to receive cashback, discounts, and special privileges on your purchases.

Subscribe to Email Newsletters and notifications: Receive unique discounts, promotions, and early access to sales events by subscribing to stores' email newsletters and notifications.

Employ Browser Extensions and Price monitoring programs: Use browser extensions and price monitoring programs to automatically apply coupons, compare prices, receive deal alerts, and watch price movements for products you're interested in.

By applying these tactics and utilizing accessible tools, customers may save money, uncover the best bargains, and make intelligent purchasing decisions when shopping online. With a little time and effort, it's feasible to optimize savings and enjoy a more satisfying online shopping experience.

THE END

www.ingramcontent.com/pod-product-compliance
Lightning Source LLC
Chambersburg PA
CBHW070048260726
48658CB00002B/790